ADULT SKILLS → Literacy for Living

Punctuation – Book 3

Written by Dr Nancy Mills and Dr Graham Lawler

The Adult Skills Range

The range of Adult Skills resources has been developed by Aber Education in response to needs expressed by tutors, students and governmental agencies. The materials are appropriate for adults who require support in advancing their literacy and numeracy skills.

Dr Nancy Mills, Adult Literacy/Numeracy author and editor, has over 25 years of combined experience in the adult education areas of teaching, tutor training, developing curriculum resources and publishing. Dr Graham Lawler, Adult Literacy/Numeracy author and editor, has over 27 years of combined experience in the adult education areas of teaching, tutor training, developing curriculum resources and publishing.

Adult Skills - Punctuation - Book 3

ISBN 978-1-84285-112-8

© 2009 Aber Publishing

P.O. Box 225

Abergele

Conwy County LL18 9AY

Published in Europe by Aber Publishing. www.aber-publishing.co.uk

Cover illustration by Michelle Cooper

Typesetting by Jonathan Bennett and Aber Publishing

Contents

Introduction

General

This resource, Book 3 in a series of three, deals with the use and application of basic punctuation. It is written at an approximate reading level of years 8-9, with more challenging activities than Books 1 and 2. Depending on the level of the student, it can be used following the completion of Book 2 to reinforce skills, or as a standalone resource.

Book 3 provides:

- a progression of punctuation skills,
- exercises for skills practice and development,
- summary pages for revision and reference,
- blackline masters for multiple use.

Using these materials, tutors can provide:

- focus and goals,
- modeling sessions,
- practice and feedback.

This resource can be used for:

- individual or small group lessons,
- individual practice and revision,
- take home practice.

Lessons can be used:

- in the sequence they appear in the book,
- as starters for a focus on one of the skills,
- to collect baseline information for individual students,
- as pre- or post-tests, before or after the study of a particular skill.

These skills facilitate the development of:

- reading,
- writing,
- self-confidence in putting pen to paper.

Using this resource

What is punctuation? – page 7

Before launching into activity sheets on punctuation marks, it is important that students understand the purposes and uses of punctuation. If they don't know the term punctuation, they will certainly recognise some of the punctuation marks. The first step is to ensure that they relate the word punctuation to the various marks.

A discussion of the purpose of punctuation in general, with spoken or written examples, is relevant at this point. "Why punctuate? How does punctuation help us understand what we read?"

Once students have grasped the general concept of punctuation, ask them to think of all the punctuation marks they can. Ask them to write down their definition of punctuation. Discuss their answers.

Ask questions so that you can determine if they have understood the importance of punctuation marks and are ready to move to their use. Work with each student as they fill in the blanks. Students also should become familar with the use of capital letters when using punctuation.

Punctuation – summary – page 8

This page has been included as a summary sheet or for use as a wall chart. It could be used:

- after the activity to reinforce the concept,
- after the punctuation pages and the 'What is punctuation?' discussion have been completed.

Note: This resource includes a summary for each of the seven punctuation marks introduced. They can all be used as described above.

What is a complete sentence? – pages 9-10

This page is helpful to solicit the students' understanding of sentences. If working in a small group, ideas can be shared, accepted and returned to after the sentence sheets have been completed. The activity can be used as a pre- and post-test to gauge student progress.

Capital letters and fullstops – pages 11-14

Use these three pages to review the concept of a complete sentence and reinforce the use of capital letters and fullstops.

The exercises can be used:

- as a one-on-one or small group exercise for general discussion. Is each one a sentence? If so, why? If not, why not?,
- as a follow-up exercise for revision,
- to correct the punctuation by putting in the capital letter or a fullstop, or both,
- to complete the idea to make it a sentence.

After the student has ticked the complete sentences, the activities may be used again by the students to make the other sentences complete.

The purpose of page 6 is to give examples of additional uses of capital letters. The activities will help to reinforce the use of all three concepts that have been introduced:

- complete sentences,
- fullstops,
- capital letters.

Page 13 has stories with no punctuation marks. Ask students to make corrections to any or all of the stories. These can be used as a one-on-one or small group activity. They provide an opportunity for students to discuss where and why sentences begin or end in certain places, and to justify their ideas. The groups can be of mixed or similar ability.

The summary (page 8) can be used in the same ways as suggested for page 2.

Joined sentences and paragraphs – page 15

Before students fully understand sentence structure and punctuation, their writing may be full of joined ideas using words such as and, but and then. Joining sentences in this way is easier than forming new sentences. Use this page with students to improve their writing.

Question marks and exclamation marks – pages 16-20

The purpose of these pages is to get students thinking about other punctuation marks used in sentences and the reasons for their use. As part of the activity, they could either write a sentence that requires a ! or a ?, or find an example in a book or story you provide.

The activities give practice in recognising and using question marks and exclamation marks.

The summary can be used in the same ways as suggested for page 8.

Joined sentences – page 15

Before students fully understand sentence structure and punctuation, their writing may be full of joined ideas using and, then and but. Joining sentences in this way is common for those who do not grasp basic punctuation concepts. Use this page with students to improve their writing.

Question marks and exclamation marks – page 16–19

The purpose of these pages is to get students thinking about other punctuation marks used in sentences and the reasons for their use. As part of the activity, they could either write a sentence that requires a ! or a ?, or find an example in a book or story you provide. The activities give practice in recognising and using question marks and exclamation marks.

Speech marks – pages 21-24

These pages have been developed to provide a staged introduction to punctuating with speech marks.
- Examples of why speech marks are used are presented. There is also an activity that requires students to underline the spoken parts of a fully punctuated sentence.

- The idea of beginning each new speaker on a new line is introduced. Conversations are provided for the students to read and punctuate to show their understanding.

- The rest of the activities deal with the other punctuation involved in speaking and the placement of the punctuation marks that have been introduced to this point.

Commas – more uses – page 25–27

This section introduces the placement of commas in lists of nouns and describing words, and to indicate a pause in the reading. The exercises will reinforce this use of commas.

Apostrophes – possession – page 28

The placement of possessive apostrophes is more difficult. It is a tricky concept and one that people of all ages find hard to use properly. Mastery will need time, revision and practice.
Apostrophes practice – missing letters and possession – page 25.
Examples and activities will help to reinforce the two uses of apostrophes.

Apostrophes – missing letters – page 32

The use of apostrophes in shortened words is usually logical to students and easy to grasp. There are many practice activities.

Punctuation practice – pages 34–36

Here are some revision activities for all the punctuation marks covered in this resource. They can also be used as a pre- or post-test. An answer key for the stories at the end of the book

What is punctuation?

What do we mean by **punctuation?**

Punctuation is . . .

Activity

Fill in each gap below by putting in the punctuation mark described.

	A fullstop is a mark that shows the end of a sentence.
	A capital letter goes at the beginning of a sentence.
	A question mark shows a question has been asked.
	An exclamation mark shows surprise, excitement, alarm or anger.
	Speech marks show spoken words.
	A comma is used for a pause in a sentence. It is also used to separate items in a list.
	An apostrophe is used to show where letters have been taken out of a word. It is also used to show ownership.

Punctuation summary

Fullstop
- at the end of a sentence

L M N W

Capital Letters
- at the beginning of sentences
- at the beginning of names of people and places
- the word **I**

Exclamation Mark
- at the end of a sentence to show surprise, alarm, anger

?

Question Mark
- at the end of a question

, or **'**

Comma
- for a pause in a sentence
- between words in a list of things
- with speech marks
- to clarify the meaning of a sentence

" " or **" "**

Speech Marks
- to show spoken words

 , or **'**

Apostrophes
- when letters have been left out to shorten a word
- when ownership needs to be shown

© 2009 Aber Publishing – Adult Skills   Punctuation - Book 2

What is a complete sentence?

We sometimes write words and sentences without being sure they say what we mean. In the box, write what is needed to make a sentence complete.

Activity 1
Find and underline the complete sentences. Put a line through incomplete sentences. In the box above, write anything new you discovered about what makes a sentence complete.

I approached the.

All at once the bird circled.

we enjoyed hiking through the hills

the elderly woman stood alone at the bus stop.

When she finally came towards me.

i wasn't sure if it was as realistic

We sloshed along the muddy paths

The wind tossed the mane of the horse about.

like the sea spray from the breaking waves

i slid across the smooth leather seat and jumped

it bounced off the wall like it was made of rubber.

The beach was closed after the clifftop landslide.

Like a rippling piece of silk.

As soon as the crowd disperses

Notify me when the application is due.

that is the sort of ceremony

Activity 1
Make corrections to each sentence above that is not complete.

A complete sentence is…

A complete sentence is a word, or group of words, which makes sense on its own.
A complete sentence has punctuation at the end, such as a fullstop.
A complete sentence starts with a capital letter.

Activity
These sentences are not complete. Rewrite them as complete sentences by adding words, capital letters, fullstops, or all three.

Suddenly, in the dark of night

_____

The waves broke evenly along the beach strewn with

_____

That we promised to visit but hadn't.

_____

Like a snake slithering through grass.

_____

We spent all day preparing for the barbeque

_____

without you i wouldn't have dared to volunteer

_____

They huddled together in the storm waiting to be

_____

i went directly to the scene of the accident to identify.

_____

he didn't call because he didn't have access to a phone

_____

he will be happy with any gift you give him.

_____

Capital letters and full stops – practice

Look at the sentences on the left in the box. Decide if they are complete sentences before you read the answers on the right.

The headlines in the paper were about the flooding in Somerset.	**Yes. This sentence begins with a capital letter and ends with a fullstop. It is a complete sentence.**
Finishing my application. Returning home.	**No. These are NOT complete sentences. They have capital letters and fullstops, but they do not make sense.**
my flat is not sufficiently big enough for four people.	**No. This does make sense, but it needs a capital letter to complete it.**
Surgery is the only answer to my mother's hip pain	**No. This does make sense, but it needs a fullstop to complete it.**

Activity 1

These stories do not have complete sentences. Add words, capital letters, and fullstops to correct the stories.

Story 1

walking home from the supermarket last week i saw a puppy sitting on the footpath i ran over to it and started stroking it after a while i started to leave but the puppy followed right behind me i kept walking each time i looked back i saw that the puppy was still bounding along behind me i told it to stay but it ignored my instructions when i arrived home it leaped up the steps and gave me a look of expectation i gave him some water in a dish while i contemplated what to do

Story 2

yesterday was our monthly morning tea to celebrate everyone with a birthday in july we were supposed to bring a plate but i forgot just before 10 am i ran to the corner shop down the street and bought a package of shortbread biscuits i put them on a plate on the table the receptionist had brought apple and walnut muffins the assistant manager brought savories which had been warmed up the human relations clerk made sandwiches with asparagus rolled up in them of course there was also a cake i was hoping that there would be some of my biscuits left over for me to have at lunchtime but they were all eaten

More about capital letters

Capitals are also used in other ways.

Names of people..................... begin with **capital letters**.	Dame Kiri Te Kanawa, Elvis Presley, Kylie Minogue
Names of places .... begin with **capital letters**.	Coromandel, France, Great Wall of China
Names of days and months .... begin with **capital letters**	Monday, Wednesday, March, October
Names of holidays .... begin with **capital letters**..............	Christmas, **New Year's D**ay, **St David's D**ay
Names of streets..................... begin with **capital letters**.	Rodeo Drive, Mangere Road, M1
Names of businesses .... begin with **capital letters**	Subway, Fonterra, Nike
Titles of books, magazines and newspapers .... begin with **capital letters**	New Idea, The Sunday Herald, The da Vinci Code
Initials................................ begin with **capital letters**	**CEO, MP, PS, DOB**
I... **I** is always a **capital letter**..............	I expect I will leave soon.

Activity
Cross out the lower case letters that should be capital and write in the correct letters.

henry's iq is higher than mine.

thanksgiving is celebrated in the us on the third thursday in november.

catcher in the rye is one of my favourite books.

i joined the gym at the ymca on saturday.

connie and jack are going to glasgow for joan's wedding.

the MOT on my car is due on the 3rd of august.

my parents gave me a subscription to the listener.

there was an explosion at the fireworks factory

tana's new suv is 4wd.

i have to meet sue at the library at 3 o'clock.

mr and mrs smith is a movie starring brad pitt.

the tenth annual addidas triathalon will be held in wales.

national travel is reducing their family fares for the christmas holidays.

the agm of our swimming club is the 10th of february.

my favourite tv show is dr who.

the first welsh savings bank made a big profit last year.

each morning i read the editorial in the daily post

Capital letters – practice

Activity
These stories do not have complete sentences or capital letters. Add capital letters and fullstops to correct them.

Story 1

we arrived at the snowdon visitor centre at 7 am with all our gear after just over two and a half hours we saw the peak before us we hiked for hours in total to reach the top of mt snowden finally we'd made it jake and i put down our packs and looked at the view we could see all the way to anglesey even though it was about 12 c. our bodies felt warm from the exerting hike we had planned this trip ever since reading a story about the mountain in the british airways inflight magazine on our way back from holiday months before what a wonderful way to spend new years day

Story 2

the goldenhorse concert was scheduled for May 5, May day this year, in the opera house the tickets were to go on sale at the devon street entrance at 8 am friday morning tom said he would get there early and buy tickets for him, shirley, coralee and myelf i told him to get the best seats he could when he got there the queue had about two hundred people in it already it stretched all the way to ronald street there was a news crew from tv one filming the crowds after tom got the tickets he rang me to say that i should watch eyewitness news at 6 on channel one when i turned it on i saw tom waving at the camera i couldn't hear him but i could easily read his lips when he said hi to me

Story 3

no-one believes me but i saw a ghost last night i was trying to get to sleep in nana burke's bed at the old farmhouse in devon we were visiting for the weekend granddad phil had died in this bed last april nana let my brother ben and i have her bed it was midnight and the clock chimed twelve ben was fast asleep all of a sudden i heard the door creak and then footsteps i was too scared to even open my eyes but i am certain that granddad phil was in the room watching us after what seemed like several hours ben woke up and i told him what happened he just turned over and went back to sleep and so did i but i'll never forget that experience

Capital letters – summary

Capital letters are used for:

• names of people

Dame Kiri Te Kanawa
Elvis
Presley
Winston Churchill

• the names of places

The Eiffel Tower
France
Great Wall of China

• the names of days and months

Monday
Wednesday
March
October

• the names of holidays

Christmas Day
Labour Day
New Year's day

• names of streets

Rodeo Drive
Manchester Road
Bryn Aber

• names of businesses

Subway
Fonterra
Nike

• titles of books, magazines and newspapers

New Idea
The Sunday Herald
The da Vinci Code

• initials

CEO
MP
PS
DOB

Joined sentences and paragraphs

Even the best writers sometimes write stories with several sentences joined together. They use joining words such as **then**, **so**, **but** or **and**. Too many of these joining words make writing sound repetitive and clumsy. It can make it hard to understand the meaning.

Activity 1

Correct this story. Delete the unnecessary joining words and add capital letters and fullstops.

last week my flatmate hemant and i went for a walk along blacks beach on boxing day and we wanted to collect driftwood for the garden at our flat and half way along the beach we saw a toyota station wagon that was stuck in the sand and the tyres were already covered and the tide was coming in but there was no one around but as we were looking inside we saw three kittens in a macdonalds chips box in the back and just as we were deciding how to rescue them we heard the siren of the local fire brigade and soon one of the firemen had opened the car and was removing the box of kittens then handing it to a young woman and she looked more relieved seeing her kittens than watching her car being towed to safety but we never did find out how she had gotten herself into such a predicament

What is a paragraph?

In long stories, the story is usually broken up into groups of sentences called paragraphs.

- A paragraph is usually made up of more than one sentence.
- A new paragraph is started when something new is introduced, such as a person, a place, or a change of idea or time.
- Each sentence in a paragraph is about the same topic or idea.

Activity 2

Read the story again. Indicate where each new paragraph should start by writing this symbol:

eg …to the end of his run. While he was running, Judy was…

Activity 3

Write the main idea for each paragraph that you have indicated in the story.

_____   _____

_____   _____

_____   _____

Question marks and exclamation marks

Capital letters and fullstops are common types of punctuation because they appear in most sentences.

There are two other punctuation marks that can be used in place of fullstops. They show that a sentence has ended but carry a different meaning than a fullstop.

Activity
Complete these boxes.

?	**What it means:**
	Write 3 examples:

!	**What it means:**
	Write 3 examples:

Question Marks

The question mark shows that a question was asked. We know if a sentence is a question because it needs an answer.

Activity 1

Read each of these sentences. If it is a question, turn the fullstop into a question mark.

Can I come over to your place to watch the rugby match.

When will you hear if you got the job.

My brother asked me to babysit for his children this afternoon.

Will you make tea for us tomorrow night.

I asked myself which video would be most suitable.

When you go to the supermarket would you purchase some milk.

When you mix colours does it make an interesting effect.

At which accommodation is the touring team going to stay.

He looked questioningly around the room.

What do you think the cause of the accident was.

She glanced anxiously at her watch and wondered if she was late.

Will you let me borrow your sleeping bag for the weekend.

She asked if I thought we should cancel our tennis game due to the storm.

Activity 2

Write 6 sentences of your own that are questions.

_____

_____

_____

_____

_____

_____

© 2009 Aber Publishing – Adult Skills   Punctuation - Book 2

Exclamation marks

! The exclamation mark shows that a sentence was shouted, said strongly, in surprise or alarm.

Activity 1
Read each of these sentences. Insert exclamation marks where you think they are appropriate.

Pick that up right now.

I think the new CD is absolutely terrific.

The dogs galloped along the beach disturbing the seagulls.

After three attempts I was successful on my driver's licence.

Cautiously he ascended the stairs.

Watch out for that truck.

My parents are taking possession of their new vehicle tonight.

I was so angry when a pickpocket stole my wallet at the subway station.

He nearly fell out of the window when they were joking around.

I told you **not** to cut that tree down.

Pat enrolled at art college to do a diploma in graphic arts.

Alan scored a record four tries in the match.

Low tide was at 4 am this morning.

For the first time ever, a large pod of Humpback whales was observed in the vicinity of Cardigan Bay.

We watched as the demolition team imploded the condemned building.

My grandfather's house was demolished in the flood.

I expect you to have fed the cat by the time I arrive home.

Activity 2
Write 6 sentences of your own that need a exclamation mark.

_____

_____

_____

_____

_____

_____

© 2009 Aber Publishing – Adult Skills   Punctuation - Book 2

Question marks and exclamation marks

Activities

Read these stories. Insert the correct punctuation marks, including fullstops, question marks, exclamation marks and capital letters.

Cross out any joining words that aren't needed.

Story 1

one evening my mates and i were talking about going somewhere over easter weekend but where should we go then after discussing it for a few minutes we decided to go hiking so we agreed that we would go to lundy island in the bristol channel

and the day of departure came and we gathered our gear which included backpacks, hiking boots, rain gear and sleeping bags but did we know anyone we could borrow a tent from and we could only find a 10-man size to borrow but we finally found a friend with a 4-man tent

so we met at my flat in wellington in somerset and drove to the minehead ferry terminal to make the crossing to lundy but when we got there we found that the crossing had been cancelled due to gale force winds and huge waves and we were so disappointed but we decided to wait for the weather to improve and we waited for six hours

and finally we knew we would have to cancel the trip because we needed at least two days to do the trip so that we could get home by monday evening because we all had to go to work on tuesday morning and so we hopped in our car and we drove home and unpacked

then we had a cup of tea and talked about our aborted trip like when we should reschedule our queen charlotte walk so we decided that we would do it over waitangi day weekend when the weather would surely be better

Story 2

last christmas was the first time i decided to get organised and make a list of the people i wanted to buy gifts for and what i wanted to buy everyone and how much i wanted to spend

so i wrote down all the names and then got adverts from stores like the warehouse, farmers, arbuckles and mitre 10 and i looked through them and tried to find things that i thought everyone would like but could i afford all the things i wrote down

so i added up the totals to be sure i wasn't over my budget and i it was twice what i had to spend and it took me hours to redo my list

then i set aside one day in early december to go to each store and buy what i had written down and i was so surprised that i managed to get all my shopping done because in the past i was still shopping on christmas eve but when will i ever get all these presents wrapped

Question marks and exclamation marks – summary

?

Use a **question mark** to show that a question has been asked.

We know if a sentence is a question because it needs an answer.

!

The **exclamation mark** shows that a sentence was shouted, said strongly, excitedly, in surprise or alarm.

?

Has your sister had her baby yet?

What time does the concert begin?

Where is the closest supermarket?

How many times have you driven to Wellington in Somerset?

!

Move out of the way!

You are **not** to speak to your mother that way!

We just can't wait until we move in to our new house.

I never thought so many people would be at the concert!

That train nearly ran into us!

Speech marks

Speech marks are sometimes called **quotation marks**.

In many stories, spoken words are written.

Speech marks go at the beginning and end of spoken words to show the exact words that have been said.

Each time a new person speaks, the words start on a new line.

In these examples, study the underlined, spoken words and the placement of the speech marks.

> "<u>What time does the movie start</u>?" Marie asked.
>
> I told her that it would start in an hour.
>
> "<u>I hope we aren't going to be late</u>," she said worriedly. "<u>We have to find a place to park and buy our tickets</u>."
>
> "<u>OK, then. Let's leave right now</u>," I suggested, but I knew we would have plenty of time to spare.

Activity 1

In this story, Richard and Jill are speaking to each other. Underline only the words they actually say. The first one is done for you.

"<u>I got these new hiking boots last night</u>," said Richard proudly.

Jill admired them and said, "They're brilliant."

"I've wanted them for a long time. With my new job, I was able to buy the ones I really wanted," said Richard.

Jill inquired, "How much did they cost?"

Richard told her that the regular price was £59.99 but they were on sale for a 25% discount.

"So, how much did they cost?" she repeated. "I might want to purchase a pair for myself."

"I paid £45.00 for them," Richard said patiently. "Don't you know what 25% off £59.99 is?"

"Of course I do! I just wanted to make sure you didn't pay too much," she chided.

Activity 1

Circle all the speech marks in the sentences above.
Are they at the beginning and the end of each of the underlines you drew?

© 2009 Aber Publishing – Adult Skills   Punctuation - Book 2

Commas used with speech marks

Here is part of the conversation from the previous page:

> **"I got these new tramping boots last night," said Richard proudly.**
>
> **Jill admired them and said, "They're brilliant."**

In this example, you can see that a comma goes:

• right <u>after</u> the words have been said in the first sentence, and

• right <u>before</u> the words have been said and before the speech marks in the second sentence.

> **"I've wanted them for a long time. With my new job, I was able to buy the ones I really wanted," said Richard.**

In this example, you can see that when two or more sentences are spoken together, the speech marks are placed at the *beginning* **of the first sentence and** *end* **the last sentence.**

"I paid £45.00 for them," I said patiently. "Don't you know what 25% off £59.99 is?"

In this example, two spoken sentences are separated by words that are not spoken. Speech marks are placed *before* **and** *after* **the words in each spoken sentence.**

Activity 1
Put speech marks, fullstops, commas and question marks in the correct places in these sentences.

Did you see the notice about the company Christmas party asked Judith We are playing war games.

Yes It sounds like fun replied Mike

Judith said curiously Are you going to go

Mike thought for a minute Finally he admitted I've never played Wargames before. It sounds a bit violent

Judith recalled her experience for a minute before answering The semi-automatic weapons shoot red dye pellets that make a mess on your shirt but don't hurt I played it once where I worked before I came here

Other than having some fun, what is the point Mike continued

It's supposed to be good for team building Judith explained You plan strategies and look after each other

Well Mike asked candidly can you get shot by your own team There are certainly some people at work who would love to do that to me

Don't be worried Mike Remember that it's only a game laughed Judith.

Punctuation in a conversation

Activities

Study each of these photographs. Make up the people's names and write a conversation they might be having that goes with the photo.

Use all of the punctuation marks you have learned:

capital letters   .   ?   !   ,   " "

1.

2.

Speech marks – summary

"   "

Speech marks go at the beginning and end of what a person says.

Use a comma after the words have been said:

"Let me know when you are ready to go," reminded Steph.

Use a comma after the speaker is mentioned.

Mary answered, "I'll ring you in the morning."

"   "

When several people are speaking, each person's words are on a new line. When two or more sentences are spoken, the speech marks are placed at the beginning and end of what was said.

Stuart agreed, "OK, but don't make it too early."

"I'll ring at 8 am, then," Mary said, thinking he Stuart would be happy.

"At that time I won't even be out of bed," he confessed.

"   "

When two sentences are spoken by one person, but separated by words that are not spoken, speech marks are placed before and after the spoken words.

"I can't believe that you don't get up until 9 am," admitted Mary. "You must go to bed really late?"

"I usually go to bed after midnight", he admitted. "I'm a night owl."

?   !

A question mark or exclamation mark can also be used with spoken words.

"Can't you get up a bit earlier tomorrow?" Mary inquired, somewhat annoyed.

Stewart demanded, "Just tell me why you want to ring me at 8 am!"

"Don't you want me to wish you a happy birthday before I leave for work?" Mary asked.

"Is that what this is about?" thought Stewart. "OK, just this once, then."

"Great!" Mary exclaimed, "I'll even sing the birthday song to you."

Commas – more uses

Commas are used:

•   in speaking to separate what is said from who said it.

There are three more uses for commas.

CORRECT **Don't forget to take your binoculars, sand shoes, sunhat and sunblock on the whale watch trip.**	A comma is used to separate items in a list.
CORRECT **The sea was blue, deep, choppy and cold.**	Commas are also used to separate lists of adjectives - words that describe something.
NOT CORRECT **On the trip I was excited, thrilled, exhausted, and, impressed.**	A comma is not placed between the last item or adjective in the list, or after the words *and* and *or*.
CORRECT **Once we got back to shore, everyone went for a coffee.**	A comma is used to mark a place in a sentence to make you pause.

Activities

1. Put commas in these lists of items.

Please don't turn on the TV listen to the radio play a CD or sing out loud.

Are we going to eat at Grumpy Tom's Black Angus Steakhouse BBQ Heaven or The Hub?

You'd better have your oil water brake fluids and battery water checked.

Let's order sausages salad beer chips and something for dessert.

The movers are taking the fridge beds sofa kitchen table TV and bookcase.

2. Put the commas in these lists of adjectives.

Her helpful concerned patient and generous friends supported her through the tragedy.

My new job is interesting challenging and demanding but well-paid.

That spider is black ugly hairy poisonous and disgusting!

The recovered Creedo bike was scratched dented rusty and a total wreck!

3. Put the commas in these sentences where the reader should pause.

Whatever you do don't consider shifting to Ireland.

In the summer scores of tornadoes are observed in the US.

At morning tea coffee and donuts were served.

The woman with the injured baby in her arms cried for help.

Commas – more uses

Commas are used:

- in writing to separate what is said from who said it
- to separate lists of items
- to separate lists of adjectives
- to make the reader pause

Commas are also used to make the meaning of a sentence clear.

NOT CORRECT
On Monday the first, guests arriving.

CORRECT
On Monday, the first guests are arriving.

If a comma is put in the wrong place, a sentence are can give an unintended meaning.

NOT CORRECT
As the traffic passed by the accident victims were being treated by the paramedics.

CORRECT
As the traffic passed by the accident, victims were being treated by the paramedics.

If a comma is left out, a sentence can also give a wrong or confusing meaning.

Activity

Remove or add commas in these sentences so that they are not confusing and give the meaning you think is correct.

Before you leave the dishes need putting away.

Last year I met the guy, who I later married on the Internet.

The weather reports, of which are ominous, may ruin our picnic.

The used desk with drawers, full of pencils paper clips and food scraps was disgusting.

I rang Sylvia invited her over watched for her through the window and greeted her at the door.

I thought until December, that I didn't have any leave left.

After my child is born I believe I won't get any sleep for weeks.

Tourists who travel frequently get lots of airpoints.

Babies who have stomach aches daily should see a doctor.

Sunday will be fine, and windy, later in the day.

My fiancé is a fun loving and happy person.

The electrician, fixed the exposed wires standing on a ladder.

Commas – more uses

Commas are used:

- in writing to separate what is said from who said it,
- to separate lists of items,
- to separate lists of adjectives,
- to make the reader pause and give sentences meaning,
- to give sentences meaning

Four more uses of commas are:

- to separate the parts of a sentence that begin as a statement and end as a question,
- to highlight extra information,
- to tell when, where or how something happened,
- to separate a word or words at the beginning, middle or end of a sentence that could be left out without changing the general sense of the sentence.

You have finished preparing for exam, haven't you? **When the accountant's report is ready, let me know.**	**A comma separates parts of a sentence.**
The elephant, *followed by the baby,* **was nearly killed by poachers.** **Did the horse,** *with the female jockey,* **win the race?**	**A comma can be used to highlight extra information.**
The boy, *in the middle of the night,* **walked out into the freshly fallen snow and disappeared.**	**A comma can be used to tell when, where or how something happened.**
Her aunt, *nearly 90 years old,* **fell and broke her hip.**	**A comma can be used to describe someone or something.**
There were no parking places left, *however.* **I went early,** *also,* **to ensure I had a seat.**	**A comma can be used to separate words that could be left out, without changing the meaning of the sentence.**
Unfortunately, **the game was rained out.**	**The words that could be left out can be at the beginning, middle, or end of the sentence.**
The game, *unfortunately,* **was rained out.**	
The game was rained out, *unfortunately.*	

Putting it altogether - practice

Activity 1

Add commas in these sentences so that they give the meanings you think are correct.

The graduation will be finished noon won't it?

If it snows tomorrow all schools will be closed won't they?

She's bought her wedding gown hasn't she?

Are the children playing in the park ready to go home?

Will the members sitting in the back pews please move to the front?

Have the cars purchased in Chester arrived yet?

His hiking boots wet from his fall in the river are drying on the rock.

The artist who was French painted colourful abstracts.

My tutor new at the beginning of the term has scheduled a quiz for tomorrow.

This is a chance for you to use all of the punctuation marks you have learned, including how to decide when a new paragraph should be started.

Activity 2

In this story, all the joining words have been left out. However, sometimes joining words are useful. Insert joining words, paragraph marks, capital letters and all the punctuation marks needed to correct this story.

before world war i jobs for unmarried women were usually limited to domestic service or women's industries and they include tailoring leatherwork and footwear but after marriage most women stayed home and cared for their children and husbands but for many women world war i brought the opportunity to work in a variety of new jobs and often they took over the jobs of their husbands brothers or fathers some positions had special names for example garage attendants were called petrol nymphs and road sweepers were called street housemaids women working in munitions and engineering factories were called the munitionettes and it was common for women to be treated as inferior to men earning lower wages but working longer hours so the women's army auxiliary corps (waac) was set up in 1917 and this freed more men to go to war the women's royal naval service (wrns) and the women's royal auxiliary air force (wraff) were formed soon after and in 1917 the women's land army was formed this organisation was designed to help farms whose male workers had gone to war and was especially necessary after food rationing was introduced so during world war i women enjoyed the new independence and comradeship that work offered them even though some jobs were hard and not particularly pleasant women came to believe that the view of 'a woman's place is in the home' was changing

Punctuation - Book 2

Commas – summary

! ! ! !

Commas are used:

- **to separate what is said from who said it.**

"I have tickets for next Saturday," revealed Jay.

"I can't wait for the concert," Chris replied, "but remember I'm driving."

- **to separate items in a list.**

Throw away the mouldy vegetables, spoiled milk, smelly meat and melted ice-cream.

- **to separate lists of adjectives.**

The child was cranky, stubborn, frustrated and miserable.

- **to mark a place in a sentence to indicate a pause for the reader.**

She edited the report she had written, on the airplane.

- **to make the reader pause and give sentences meaning.**

The members, who were in the band, arrived early.

- **to separate the parts of a sentence that begin as a statement and end as a question.**

She tried on the dress before she bought it, didn't she?

- **to highlight extra information**

Peter's grandmother, frightened by a diving magpie, ran for cover.

- **to tell when, where or how something happened**

Several rugby players, during Saturday's match, got sent to the blood bin.

- **to separate a word or words in a sentence, at the beginning, middle or end, that could be left out without changing the general sense of the sentence.**

Finally, the crowd dispersed without making a scene.

The young kitten, unfortunately, got stuck under the sofa.

I felt that I should attend the funeral, however.

Apostrophes – missing letters

Apostrophes can be used:

- in place of a letter or letters to shorten or abbreviate words.

  For example: *I am* can be shortened to *I'm*.

In these words, called contractions, the apostrophe is placed where the letter or letters are taken out.

have not = haven't	I will = I'll

Activity
Make contractions out of each word and write a sentence using them.

I have_____

is not _____

we have _____

has not _____

they have _____

have not _____

he is _____

cannot _____

she is _____

would not _____

we are _____

should not _____

they are _____

let us _____

I will _____

I would _____

we will_____

we would_____

you will _____

you would _____

they will _____

they would_____

Apostrophes – possession

Two more uses of **apostrophes** are:

*   to show that something belongs to one person or thing.

    For example: *This itinerary was prepared for Kim . = This is Kim's itinerary.*

The apostrophe goes before the *s* to show the itinerary belongs to one person, Kim.

*   to show that something belongs to more than one person or thing.

    For example: *The girls bought bouquets. = These are the girls' bouquets.*

The apostrophe goes after the *s* to show the bouquets belong to more than one girl.

Using apostrophes to show possession.

I bought Ellie a new subscription.	**The apostrophe goes before the** *s*
It is Ellie's subscription.	**because Ellie is one person.**
The CDs belong to my sons.	**The apostrophe goes after the** *s*
They are my sons' CDs.	**because there is more than one son.**

Activity

Look at the pictures below and ask yourself, "Who does it belong to?
If it belongs to one person, the apostrophe goes *before* **the** *s***.**
If it belongs to more than one person, the apostrophe goes *after* **the** *s***.**

Examples:

Here is a cat with stripes.

The cat's stripes.

Here are three cats with stripes.

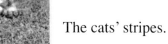

The cats' stripes.

Activity

Write a sentence for each word showing possession of the item by one person or thing, and write a second sentence showing possession of the item by more than one person or thing.

farmers/gumboots _____

farmers/gumboots _____

musicians/instrument _____

musicians/instruments_____

teams/gear _____

teams/gear _____

grandparents/ancestors _____

grandparents/ancestors _____

Apostrophes practice
– missing letters, possession

Activity 1 Missing letters
1. In the blank, write a word with an appropriate contraction.

According to the schedule, _____ due to arrive any minute. _____ saved for his

overseas experience for two years. You _____ notified me when the smoke alarm went off.

_____ a good idea to start training several months in advance. He _____returned the

items he borrowed and _____ starting to wonder if _____ get them back before I go on my

trip. When _____ finished their training, _____ go to their first match.

If _____ just agree to let me drive, _____ sure you _____ be disappointed.

The building _____ strong enough to endure _____ first earthquake and, unfortunately,

it was destroyed.

Activity 2 Possessives
2. Write in the apostrophe in the appropriate places in each sentence.

When will the security guards shift end?

When will the security guards shifts end?

The athletes perspiration was drenching his shirt.

The athletes perspiration was drenching their shirts.

The reports, written by each managers personal assistant, were required to have sections on safety
procedures.

The reports, written by all the managers personal assistants, were required to have a section on safety
procedures.

The drivers errors caused cars to crash on the track.

Many drivers errors caused cars to crash on the track.

My friends application was returned without comment.

My two friends applications were returned without comment.

Tsunamis destruction can be devastating.

The tsunamis destruction devastated several beaches.

Apostrophe – summary

> ❜

- An **apostrophe** is used to shorten two words to make one word.

  are not   =   aren't

- An **apostrophe** is inserted in where the letter(s) have been taken out.

  let us   =   let's

> ❜

- An **apostrophe** is used to show that something belongs to someone or something.

The kitten belongs to Sara.
It is *Sara's* kitten.

The motorcycle has a punctured tyre.
It is the motorcycle's punctured tyre.

> ❜

- An **apostrophe** is used to show that something belongs to more than one person or thing.

The musicians have their music. It is the musicians' music.

The buildings have leaks.
They are the buildings' leaks.

The cat's stripes.

The cats' stripes.

Punctuation practice 1

> **.** Use a **fullstop** at the end of all other sentences.
>
> **?** Use a **question mark** in a sentence that asks a question.
>
> **!** Use an **exclamation mark** in a sentence that is said strongly.

1. Read the sentences below.
   For each sentence, write in one of the three punctuation marks above.

The plane is departing three hours late

What expectations do you have for length of the exam

Be sure to tell me when your baby is due

How many hours per week do you attend night classes

Do you have personal medical insurance

On Friday the 13th a black cat ran across in front of me

How many dependent children do you have in your care

The universe contains billions of galaxies of different shapes and sizes

Powered flight developed rapidly from the early 1900s

Do you believe that man has landed on the moon

Discuss any experiences you have had with the supernatural

How many times does an average resting heart beat per minute

> **.** Use a **fullstop** at the end of a complete sentence.
>
> **C** Use a **capital** to start the names of people, places and days.
>   The word **I** is always a capital letter.

2. **Decide on the punctuation each sentence needs.**
   For each sentence, write in one of the punctuation marks above.

the kayapo is one of the five hundred different amerindian tribes

in 1954 a soviet rocket reached the outer atmosphere and launched the sputnik satellite into orbit around the earth

les miserables is a musical that has been performed all over the world for the last twenty years

the titanic, built in ireland, was the largest and most modern of all passenger ships of the time

on st patricks day, our family would often go to a a st patricks day parade

tai chi is an ancient system of physical movement developed in china thousands of years ago

down syndrome is a condition which causes slower than normal mental, motor and language abilities

on 26 december 2004, a 9.0 magnitude earthquake occurred in the indian ocean

jfk airport is one of the largest and busiest in the us

one performer in cirque de lumineaux is the famous gymnast gary wells

Punctuation practice 2

> , Use a **comma** to separate lists of adjectives.
>
> , Use a **comma** to mark a place in a sentence to make the reader pause.
>
> , Use a **comma** to give sentences meaning.

1. Put the commas in the correct places in these sentences.

Winter can bring cold nights crisp days rain hail and snow.

Babies like some adults aren't happy when their schedules are interrupted.

The restaurant specialises in breakfast coffee light meals and desserts.

During the interview I felt nervous tense stressed and unqualified.

This itinerary looks complete doesn't it?

In the meantime why don't you ask your mother to live with you?

The appointment was postponed due to lack of interest until next month.

Next week at 7.30pm on Thursday there will be a new programme on TV.

On Saturday weather permitting we're hiking to the top of the mountain.

> " " Use **speech marks** around the words someone says.
>
> , Use **commas** to separate what is said from who said it.

2. Insert or correct the punctuation in each sentence.

Expect to be surprised my brother told me three days before my birthday.

After reading the excerpts from the book Josh explained I decided to buy it.

We are planning a demonstration Sue said It will be on Friday at 10 am.

When I asked him which road to take Ed said that Devon Street would be best.

The car came out of nowhere I exclaimed If I hadn't been quick it would have hit me.

Does anyone want the last piece of cake I asked as if I didn't know.

No matter when you get home my mum requested wake me up.

When they told me the plane had just departed I said I didn't care.

Why does it always happen Jill pondered that I am the last person to be invited

3. Write in the apostrophes thart are needed in each sentence.

Weve come a long way since Wright brothers invention.

The factorys employees are going on strike tomorrow morning, arent they?

Three families junk will be combined for the garage sale.

Werent Tinas aunties visiting from the Philippines?

Its time the chefs knives were sharpened as hes having trouble cutting the carrots.

George couldve bought the ten acres hed wanted but he left it too long.

I know that Mathewll be pleased when his clients accounts are paid.

My mothers false teeth got thrown out with yesterdays garbage.

Ken hadnt considered the implications of his girlfriends threat.

Punctuation practice 3

In these two stories there are a lot of missing punctuation marks. There are also too many ands, thens and buts. Make all the corrections and then copy the story on a separate page. Remember to use paragraphs.

Story 1

when i got home from work on tuesday there was a strange suv outside my flat but unsure of whose it was i hurried inside opened the front door and there sitting having a cup of tea was uncle tom then impulsively i ran and threw my arms around him nearly spilling his tea uncle tom i exclaimed what are you doing in wales i thought you were in the us i got home last night after a twelve hour flight he explained for the next two hours he told me about some of his experiences and he had camped in several different national parks including yellowstone the grand canyon and monument valley i took hundreds of photos would you be interested in seeing them when theyre ready he asked of course i would uncle tom i assured him someday i hope to take a journey just like youve done and uncle tom stayed at my place for a couple of hours talking non-stop about his trip and some of the people he met i reckon you could write a book about all your adventures i suggested if i took time to write a book i wouldnt have time to do all the travelling ive planned

Story 2

ever since i was a child i loved assembling model airplanes so when my son gave me one for christmas i couldnt contain my excitement there are hundred of pieces to put together joel explained how long do you think itll take you to put it together and i thought for a moment and knew what he was getting at itd probably go a lot quicker if you helped dont you think and the smile on his face was worth a million dollars well then shouldnt we get started he replied running to clear the table the picture of the vintage world war ii spitfire designed by reginald mitchell and made by supermarine was on the front of the box but it wasnt hard to imagine it flying through the air chasing enemy aircraft getting into dogfights and then scurrying back to base although not all pilots made it back and then we sat down and i studied the models instructions carefully joel was anxiously waiting for his first task find and open the packet labelled group A i stipulated place them in group As container and he painstakingly did this with each packet in the box then after two hours he was beginning to tire but i have to admit that my eyes were sore my head was throbbing and my back was aching from the concentration lets put this away for now joel i proposed itll still be here tomorrow wont it then at 7 am the next morning my sons determination led him to my bedroom to drag me back to the table arent we going to have breakfast first i queried the stores boxing day sales are on today dad if we hurry and get this finished we can buy another for half price and this made me chuckle i knew that it would take at least several hours work to put the model together working by myself but with joels help probably twice that long

Punctuation practice (answers to page 36) !!!!

Story 1

When I got home from work on Tuesday, there was a strange SUV outside my flat. Unsure of whose it was, I hurried inside, opened the front door and there, sitting having a cup of tea, was Uncle Tom. Impulsively I ran and threw my arms around him, nearly spilling his tea.

"Uncle Tom!" I exclaimed, "What are you doing in Wales? I thought you were in the US."

"I got home last night after a twelve hour flight," he explained. For the next two hours, he told me about some of his experiences. He had camped in several different national parks including Yellowstone, the Grand Canyon and Monument Valley.

"I took hundreds of photos. Would you be interested in seeing them when they're ready?" he asked.

"Of course I would, Uncle Tom," I assured him. "Someday I hope to take a journey just like you've done."

Uncle Tom stayed at my place for a couple of hours, talking non-stop about his trip and some of the people he met.

"I reckon you could write a book about all your adventures," I suggested.

"If I took time to write a book, I wouldn't have time to do all the travelling I've planned.

Story 2

Ever since I was a child, I loved assembling model airplanes, so when my son gave me one for Christmas, I couldn't contain my excitement.

"There are hundred of pieces to put together," Joel explained. "How long do you think it'll take you to put it together?"

I thought for a moment and knew what he was getting at. "It'd probably go a lot quicker if you helped, don't you think?" The smile on his face was worth a million dollars.

"Well then, shouldn't we get started?" he replied, running to clear the table.

The picture of the vintage World War II Spitfire, designed by Reginald Mitchell and made by Supermarine, was on the front of the box. It wasn't hard to imagine it flying through the air, chasing enemy aircraft, getting into dogfights and then scurrying back to base, although not all pilots made it back.

We sat down and I studied the model's instructions carefully. Joel was anxiously waiting for his first task. "Find, and open, the packet labelled group A," I stipulated. "Place them in group A's container."

He painstakingly did this with each packet in the box. After two hours, he was beginning to tire. I have to admit that my eyes were sore, my head was throbbing and my back was aching from the concentration.

"Let's put this away for now, Joel," I proposed. "It'll still be here tomorrow, won't it?"

At 7 am the next morning my son's determination led him to my bedroom to drag me back to the table. "Aren't we going to have breakfast first?" I queried.

"The stores Boxing Day sales are on today, Dad. If we hurry and get this finished, we can buy another for half price."

This made me chuckle. I knew that it would take at least several hours work to put the model together working by myself, but with Joel's help, probably twice that long!